RAW *for* LIFE

SUNITA VIRA
Founder of the Raw Food Center
Chicago & Singapore

Published by

www.RawFoodCentre.com

ISBN: 978-0-9997426-1-7

Library of Congress Control Number: 2017964195

Printed in the United States of America

This publication contains the opinions and ideas of the author based on the experience and research of the author. It is not intended as a substitute for consulting with your physician or other health-care provider. Any attempt to diagnose and treat an illness should be done under the direction of a health-care professional. The author and publisher are not responsible for any adverse effects or consequences resulting from the use of any suggestions, preparations, or applications of any of the contents of this book. The author and publisher disclaim all liability in connection with the use of this book.

contents

the inspiration

To our three children, Alisha, Maya and Rishi who have been the source of my inspiration over these past 20 years. They taught me, it was not enough to say it was "good for you," healthy food had to be absolutely delicious for our children to eat it and hence started my journey...

To my family, friends and clients who have encouraged me over the years to write a book, this is for you. I am grateful and blessed to have such an amazing, supportive community around me since starting the Raw Food Center in 2010. For their invaluable feedback on the recipes which are tried and tested to make them just right.

The recipes in this book are the best selection of "Quick & Easy" favorites from our home and from our regular culinary classes/programs from Chicago, Singapore and annual retreats around the world. Enjoy!

my story

I grew up on a tea plantation in Darjeeling, India. I was surrounded by fresh air, farm-to-table ingredients, and home cooking with spices that others call exotic but, to me, tasted like home. I watched my father savor the taste of his tea the same way we relished my mother's sumptuous cooking. I learned early the importance and nuance of flavor, aroma and balance.

During holiday get-togethers, my grandparents (both wonderful cooks) would challenge each other and compete for whose food tasted the best. The rest of us were happy recipients of their contest; everything on the table was delicious! Back then, I cherished meals for the laughter and love, as well as the magic on our plates. Today, I remember them for the way they connected food and eating to generosity and gratitude. Our family continues the tradition of eating together, and everyone gets in on the act. My three children are my official tasters; nothing makes it into our programs if it doesn't get a 10 (out of 10) and a super-enthusiastic thumbs-up from them. They each assist with demonstrations, and my daughter shoots our videos for our YouTube channel. (Raw Food Center) Even our dog, Alfa, gets involved...he is the only 100% raw member of the family. The children make his dehydrated kibbles from juice pulp with a blend of superfoods and oils which he loves!

In 2010, I founded The Raw Food Centre, Singapore with the mission to spread awareness about raw living foods and to work with families to integrate healthy eating into their busy lifestyles. In 2014, we expanded to Chicago and for retreats to fun locations like Bali in 2016. Through our site, we offer many culinary programs, cleanses, workshops and recipes. **www.rawfoodcentre.com**

about me

As a chef and an educator, I have a passion for getting you comfortable in the kitchen and sharing recipes and knowledge I've gained from a lifetime of learning and experimenting with foods.

As a mother, I take my inspiration from my children and I will guide those of you struggling with how to plan and prepare healthy food for yourself and your family.

As an artist, I love to experiment with ingredients and create food that is unique and looks and tastes delicious.

As a global traveler and a woman of Indian heritage, I offer you the world in terms of cuisine, flavors, spices, preparations, and techniques.

As a healer, I approach food with respect and embrace raw (or nearly raw), living, plant-based foods and methods that result in increased energy, enhanced immunity and disease prevention, effective weight management, clearer eyesight, glowing skin, thicker hair, better sleep, improved metabolism and fertility, deceleration of the aging process, and relief from depression.

I am a certified Gourmet Raw Food Chef and Nutrition Educator from the Living Light Culinary Institute and Matthew Kenney Culinary Academy in California. I am committed to making our raw journey together appealing, delicious and manageable. Having developed a new, global approach to raw cuisine, I look forward to sharing it with you.

for you

I am excited to put this book together for you. This is an accumulation of my learnings, research and countless hours of experimentation in the kitchen. My travels around the world, studying what has worked for various cultures, their wisdom, their flavors, tastes and textures all melding together. Using food as medicine. The healing foods that have worked for centuries...

But most of all, the tremendous health benefits that have come with incorporating these foods into our lifestyle. I will be the first to tell you that I am not 100% raw and you do not need to be to enjoy the health benefits. It is all about adding the good back in and eating in balance and harmony with nature. No one diet fits all, we are each unique, listen to your body. And folks, there is no magic pill! But I will tell you this, by adding these foods into our lifestyle, it has made an enormous difference is my family's heath and I want this for you too. Many of the diseases today are reversible by the foods we eat. We all have a choice to opt for expensive pharmaceuticals down the road or use food as medicine, the choice is yours...

My hope is that you use this book as a guide and pick a few recipes to take into your everyday lifestyle. Making small changes every week and over a few months, you will have huge shifts. I have divided the book into sections of breakfast, snacks, lunch & dinner, fermented foods and desserts to make it easy to navigate. The recipes in this book are quick, easy and delicious.

Food brings us together for fun, laughter, memories and health. Here's to your health!

introduction

Raw food has changed my life. I experience its undeniable benefits everyday. Raw food inspires me, grounds me, keeps me and my family well and has given me tons of energy and clarity to pursue what I thought was impossible! In this book, I will show you how quick, easy and fun it is to make healthy eating a part of your lifestyle! I can't wait for you to get started and discover the healing power of this food and experience the benefits first hand!

As a young woman, I seriously considered going into medical research. I wanted to come up with cures for diseases and be of service—to make a contribution to improving people's lives. The more I learned, the more I was not impressed by the pharmaceutical industry and I went on to study art & design.

the healing power of food

Fast forward to Sunita, a mother of two (our third would come later) eating the standard American diet and suffering from low energy, poor vision, brain fog, and baby weight that wouldn't go away. We were living in California at the time and I had a fulfilling career running a new web design firm. My first client, who is now a dear friend, introduced me to raw food through a group of 80-year-old men she worked with. They were more active and energized than men half their age! They had the brightest and whitest eyes I had seen in a long time, they were nimble and joyous—all due to eating a raw diet.

After that, I was hooked and experienced near-immediate results: my vision improved, I no longer needed my thick glasses to see and my hair got thicker, my energy went up, I lost all the baby weight and I experienced mental clarity! Since those early days, my family and I have made a 180-degree change. Our energies are consistently high and we hardly ever get sick. I realized that if my family experienced these amazing benefits, everyone would. It was then that I understood that raw food was the way I could impact people's lives for the better.

As I like to call it... "Living Food"... Forget your preconceived ideas. We are not just eating carrots & lettuce! Raw doesn't mean cold, hard and fibrous. Once you try the recipes in this book, you'll wonder whether they are cooked or raw. You'll find some very familiar dishes created using healthful techniques to optimize nutrition. You are not leaving your former kitchen behind when you embrace living foods; you are simply adding the good back into your life!

more about raw food

"It always blows me away to see the transformational benefits that our clients experience, once they incorporate more raw living foods into their lifestyle!"

Raw food can be warm, rich and abundantly flavorful. Put simply, living food is food that is not prepared over high heat (a process that can strip even the most healthful food of its essential beneficial nutrients). Food prepared at a low temperature (not exceeding 118 degrees Fahrenheit or 50 degrees Celsius) optimally retains its life-sustaining wholesomeness. Creative techniques such as blending, marinating, sprouting, fermenting and dehydrating take the place of traditional heat cooking in a living food kitchen.

PANTRY LIST

DRY

- Seeds: Sunflower, Pumpkin, Sesame, Chia & Flax
- Nuts: Almonds, Cashews, Walnuts, Pine Nuts & Macadamia Nuts
- Wild Rice
- Seaweed: Wakame, Arame, Hijiki, Dulse Flakes & Nori Sheets, Kelp Noodles
- Rice Paper
- Legumes: Mung, Red Lentil, French Lentil & Green Peas

OILS

- Coconut, Mustard, Olive & Flax Oil, Hemp Seed Oil

SWEETENERS

- Maple Syrup, Palm Sugar or Coconut Sugar, Raw Local Honey & Dates

SEASONINGS

- Chick Pea Miso
- Himalayan Pink Salt
- Apple Cider Vinegar
- Tamari (Wheat-free)
- Mixed Italian Herbs & Oregano
- Indian Spices: Indian Spices: Turmeric, Cumin & Coriander
- Paprika, Cayenne, Cinnamon, Clove, Nutmeg & Vanilla

SUPERFOODS

- Cacao
- Bee Pollen
- Vitamineral Green, Spirulina & Chlorella
- Goji Berries
- Dried White Mulberries
- Hulled Hemp Seeds
- Coconut Manna

KITCHEN ESSENTIALS

You can begin with your household kitchen equipment and add as you go:

- Blender
- Food Processor
- Juicer
- Dehydrator (optional)

Additional items to make your life easier in the kitchen:

- Mac MSK65 Santoku Dimpled Knife
- Ceramic Mandoline Slicer
- Sprout Bags & Nut Milk Bags
- Measuring Cups & Kitchen Scale
- Vegetable Peeler
- Measuring Spoons
- Cutting Board
- Knife Sharper
- Colander
- Spirooli
- Funnel
- Grater

MEAL PLANNING

Being organized is key! Preparing a few items during the weekend can help cut down on time spent in the kitchen during the week. Take a few hours to make the following, which will last for several days:

- Wash and prepare all vegetables for afternoon juices
- Make nut or seed milk that last for up to 3 days
- Freeze bananas for ice creams, smoothies and shakes
- Make a basic raw soup and store in a sealed glass jar
- Make one or two salad dressings
- Make one batch of nut/seed pate or cheese
- Make a few entreés, dehydrated snacks or desserts (such as burgers, marinara sauce for noodles, hummus, crackers, cookies etc.)
- Have plenty of fresh fruits and veggies, avocados, nuts and seeds to munch on

SAMPLE MENUS

The following meal suggestions require little advanced preparation and will leave you feeling light and healthy, yet satisfied.

Breakfast

Choose one of the following

- Fruit Smoothie
- Fresh Fruit Salad with Cashew Cream
- Chia Seeds Porridge with Berries & Walnut Milk
- Granola Cereal with Sesame Milk

Lunch & Dinner

Choose one or two of the following

- Raw Vegetable Soup
- Your Favorite Salad with Dressing
- Simple Wraps & Rolls
- Nut/Seed Pate, non-dairy Cheese, Guacamole or Hummus served on top of Salad or wrapped in a romaine lettuce and topped with sprouts
- Vegetable Juice
- Fettuccine with Marinara or Pesto Sauce

breakfast

start the day well

SMOOTHIES

Smoothies are the lifeblood of a raw living foods lifestyle. They are quick to prepare and are a great way to load up on nutrients for the entire family.

My family always starts their day with a big glass of smoothie for breakfast that keeps them going until lunch. All you have to do is blend and enjoy!

GREEN SMOOTHIE

serves 2–4

Kale is a powerhouse of nutrition, one of the healthiest vegetables around! This is a weekly breakfast favorite.

See our YouTube channel (RawFoodCenter) for a demo with my son.

Combine all ingredients in a blender and process until smooth. Serve at room temperature or chilled. Store in a sealed glass jar in the fridge. Finish on the same day.

1 1/2 cup mango or 2 bananas (fresh or frozen)

1 coconut water with tender coconut meat

Handful choice of any greens (romaine lettuce, spinach or kale)

1/4 cup mint leaves

1–2T hemp seeds

1T honey (optional)

1/2 cup water

1T flax seed oil or powder

1t vitamineral green powder

Pinch of Himalayan salt

We enjoy this at least once a week in our family to keep our immune system up. Whenever anyone has the sniffles or is feeling under the weather, this picks them right back up. Enjoy in the morning!

Blender Tips

- Always put liquids and high-water-content foods in the blender first so is easy to blend.
- Cut fruits and vegetables like apples, carrots and celery into small pieces so easier to blend.
- Add fats and oils at the end so as not to over-process.
- To clean the blender, put a drop of soap and fill with water. Secure lid and blend for a few seconds and rinse.

POST-WORKOUT SMOOTHIE

serves 2

Came up with this after my morning runs along the Chicago river. Walnuts are great for heart health. This smoothie is loaded with protein. The cinnamon is anti-inflammatory and the celery adds salt back into the body. The bananas have potassium and prevents cramping of the muscles. This smoothie also helps in muscle recovery and building!

Handful of walnuts

1/2 cup of hemp seeds

2 frozen bananas

2–3 celery sticks

1 cup water

1t cinnamon powder

1/2 cup water

1T coconut oil

Combine all ingredients in a blender and process until smooth. Sweeten with maple syrup if you like it sweeter.

NUT & SEED MILKS

Use nuts or seeds to create your own delicious milk in minutes and it will keep in the fridge for up to 2 days. Refer to the soak chart to follow soak times as they vary. In a rush you can keep them soaked in a jar of water in the fridge so it is ready to use. Thoroughly rinse until water is clear after soaking. Soaking nuts and seeds makes them easier to digest.

Soak Times

Almonds, other hard nuts	8–12 hours
Cashews	2–2 1/2 hours
Sunflower, sesame, pumpkin seeds	4–6 hours
Walnuts	1–2 hours
Pistachio, pecan, pinenut, macadamia, brazilnut, hemp seeds	Do not soak

ALMOND MILK

serves 4

1 cup raw almonds, soak for 8–12 hours, rinse & drain

4 cups purified water

3–4 pitted dates (to taste)

1t vanilla extract

1T coconut oil

Pinch of Himalayan salt

Great as a base for shakes. Almond milk is a staple and most popular in our home!

Combine all nuts and water in a blender and process until smooth. To separate the milk from the pulp, squeeze the mixture through a cloth mesh bag, nut milk bag or cheesecloth into a large bowl. Reserve the pulp (see tips below). Rinse the blender and pour the milk back, add remaining ingredients with a banana to make a banana milk shake or your favorite shake. Serve at room temperature or chilled.

Tips

- Use sealed glass jars to store unused milk in the fridge.
- The pulp can be used as a thickener for curries or you can dehydrate it and then grind it in a food processor and use it as flour. Can also be frozen.
- For seed milks like cashew and walnut milk, you do not need to separate pulp as the milk is smooth.

MANGO LASSI

serves 4

Love this on a hot summer afternoon, inspired by the Indian Lassi. The undertones of saffron and cardamom go great with mangoes. My kids love this, there are never any leftovers...

2 cups fresh almond milk

1 cup purified water

2–3 pitted dates (to taste)

1/2 to 1 cup ice

1 large ripe mango or 1 cup of frozen mangoes

1T coconut oil

Pinch of Himalayan salt

3–4 strands of saffron

1/4t cardamom powder

In a large blender jug, blend all except the water.

Blend until smooth, add water, blend.

Use bananas instead of mangoes for a delicious creamy banana lassi!

CASHEW MATCHA LATTÉ

serves 4

This is a great pick-me-up drink in the afternoon. I like it frothy over ice. The matcha powder is loaded with antioxidants!

Rinse and drain the cashew. In the blender first blend the cashews and water to make smooth cashew milk, then add rest of ingredients. Pour over ice and garnish with some matcha powder.

1 cup cashews soaked for 2 hours or more

3 cups purified water

1–2T maple syrup to taste

1/2 to 1 cup ice

1t vanilla extract

1T coconut oil

Pinch of Himalayan salt

2–3T matcha powder

CHIA SEED PORRIDGE

serves 1

Chia seeds are high in fiber, protein and in omega 3s which is great for brain development. Chia Seeds are filling and can act as an appetite suppressant. This is great for breakfast or any time of day.

In a medium size bowl add the chia seeds then the desired nut or seed milk. Let sit for 5–8 minutes. Stir occasionally as the chia seeds will gel up and thicken into a porridge consistency. Add salt and stir. Garnish with berries and drizzle with honey or maple syrup. Enjoy!

2T chia seeds

1/4–1/2 cup almond milk

1 sliced banana (optional)

Handful of seasonal berries

Pinch of Himalayan salt

Drizzle of honey or maple syrup

CASHEW OR WALNUT CREAM

makes about 1.5 cups

One of our family favorites, especially for Sunday brunch!

In a high speed blender, blend cashews with water, then add ice and blend for a smooth, thick, creamy consistency. Add more water if needed. Add all ingredients except the fruit. Pour the cashew cream into a container and chill in the fridge. Put fruits and berries in dessert glasses and scoop generous tablespoons of the cashew cream over the fruit. Garnish with any of the superfoods from the pantry list like dried mulberries, bee pollen and raw cacao nibs.

1 cup raw unsalted cashews or walnuts soak for 1–2 hours & drain

1/4 cup water

1/2 cup ice

1t vanilla extract

1T coconut oil

2T maple syrup (to taste)

Pinch of Himalayan salt

Bowl of seasonal berries and fruit

snacks & elixirs

sometimes savory
sometimes sweet

CHIPS & DIPS

For those mid afternoon cravings...

Quick snack ideas:

- Celery sticks with almond butter
- A bowl of fruits (preferable less sugary fruits)
- Fresh coconut water
- Flax crackers with guacamole or hummus
- Kale or kai lan chips
- Raw nutritional bars

KALE CHIPS

makes 1 large jar

1 large bunch of kale or kai lan

Generous drizzle of olive oil

1/2 lemon or 1 lime juice

1t Himalayan salt

1–2T maple syrup

1T nutritional yeast

Wash and dry kale leaves. De-stem kale leaves. Add all the ingredients except the nutritional yeast. Massage in until nicely coated. Adjust to your taste, if you like it more sour, add more lemon juice, or more maple syrup if you like it sweeter. Put on Teflex sheets of the dehydrator and sprinkle the nutritional yeast evenly. Dehydrate until crisp. Store in airtight glass container to keep the crispness.

Alternatively, you can make the kale chips in your oven if you do not have a dehydrator. Warm up oven to 250 C. Put the marinated kale leaves on the baking trays and leave in oven for 10 to 15 minutes until crisp, make sure not to burn.

(*Photo on previous page*)

SWEET POTATO CHIPS

makes 2 trays

2 sweet potatoes (best to use the ones that are orange inside)

1–2T coconut oil

1t Himalayan salt

Use a mandolin to thinly slice the sweet potatoes into a medium bowl. Mix with the oil and salt and toss evenly, put onto dehydrator sheets overnight. Then transfer to the mesh sheets and dry until crisp. Store in a glass airtight container.

ZUCCHINI HUMMUS

makes 2 cups

- 1 cup zucchini peeled & cut
- 3T lemon juice
- 3T olive oil
- 2 cloves garlic
- 1t agave nectar
- 1t paprika
- 1t Himalayan salt
- 1/4t ground cumin powder (optional)
- 1T tamari
- pinch cayenne
- 6T raw tahini
- 6T sesame seeds, soaked 4 hours, rinsed & drained

Blend all ingredients in the blender, except the tahini and the sesame seeds. Add sesame seeds and blend until smooth. Then add the tahini and blend again. Adjust to your taste of saltiness and garnish with olive oil, cumin powder and paprika.

WALNUT PATÉ

makes 1 cup

Did you know? You can make herb patés from seeds and nuts that are absolutely delicious and so quick to prepare!

Combine all the ingredients except the oil, onion and herbs in the food processor with the S-blade. Make sure to scrape down the side of the food processor with a rubber spatula. Transfer to a mixing bowl, stir in the parsley, oil and onion. Store in a sealed glass jar for 5 days in the fridge or lasts for up to 3 months in the freezer.

1 cup soaked walnuts (soaked for 1 hour in water and drained)

1T fresh lemon juice

1t extra-virgin olive oil

1t tamari

1/4t garlic powder

Pinch of Himalayan salt

1T minced parsley or a herb of your choice

1T minced onion

Notes

- The walnut gives this pate a nice meaty texture and feel.
- A nice variation for a seed pate is sunflower seeds.
- Enjoy a scoop of it on a salad or on a romaine lettuce.

ELIXIRS

What is an Elixir? Quite simply a clear, sweet liquid often mixed with alcohol and designed to deliver medication in a pleasing way. Our elixirs promote wellness and deliver optimal health benefits, without the alcohol! They are like magical health potions. A little goes a long way.

LIVER-BOOSTING ELIXIR

serves 1–2

Drink only 2 to 4 ounces of the juice as this is an elixir and is quite potent!

Juice all and add the lime juice.

1 beet

1 carrot

1 lime juice

1 handful of parsley

1 apple

FLU-BUSTER ELIXIR

serves 1–2

This liquid gold juice is loaded with a mega dose of vitamin C from the pineapple and orange. It is a powerful cold and flu fighter. Pineapple has the enzyme bromelain, which helps suppress coughs and loosen mucus. The fresh turmeric root is anti-inflammatory. Jalapeños eliminate sinus congestion and reduce sinus headaches. *(See photo at left.)*

Process all ingredients through a juicer and enjoy!

1 quarter fresh pineapple

1 orange peeled

3–4 fresh turmeric roots

1/2 handful cilantro

1/2 small jalapeño, seeded

WHEAT GRASS BLAST

serves 2

Wheat grass cleanses the blood, organs and gastrointestinal tract of debris. It restores alkalinity in the body and is a powerful detoxifier!

1 inch ginger root

1 apple chop

1T lemon juice

Handful of fresh wheatgrass

Juice the above and mix with lemon juice. Drink only one small shot glass portion as this is potent!

THERAPEUTIC BENEFITS OF FRUIT & VEGETABLE JUICES

Apple

Vitamins A & C, aids digestion, acts as a laxative and helps to detoxify the blood

Carrots

Vitamins A, B, C, D, E & K and functions as a body alkalizer

Celery

Quenches thirst, is good for the nerves, contains potassium and organic sodium and builds blood cells

Citrus

Vitamins C, beta carotene, calcium, magnesium and are good for the kidneys and liver

Cucumber

A diuretic, contains folic acid and calcium and is good for hair and nails

Kale & other dark leafy greens

High in chlorophyll, cleanses the kidneys and are high in calcium and protein

Tips

When preparing green juices, use the ratio of 1 part leafy greens such as kale, spinach or romaine lettuce to 3 parts fruits and vegetables such as cucumber, celery, apple and carrots. You can use lemon or ginger for flavoring. For palatability add more carrots, pineapple or apples. Try to keep the fruit ratio to a minimum just enough to make it palatable.

My favorite green juice!

Celery
Green Apples
Kale
Lemon
Spinach

lunch & dinner

each dish is a meal in itself

SOUPS & SALADS

Easy to make and great when you are busy and on the run! Make a batch, put in glass jars and take with you to the office!

CREAM OF ZUCCHINI & DILL SOUP

serves 4

This is a quick and easy soup to make chilled in the summer and warm in the winter.

Combine all ingredients in a blender except the avocado and olive oil. Process until smooth. Add the avocado, oil and 1/4 water to thin if necessary. Serve immediately if warm or chill in the fridge for at least 30 minutes. Garnish with a sprig of dill, olive oil and cayenne pepper.

- 1 zucchini peeled & chopped
- 1 1/2 cup warm water + 1/4 cup to thin if needed
- 1 celery stalk chopped
- 11/2T fresh lemon/lime juice
- 2t white chickpea miso
- 1 clove garlic
- 1/2t salt to taste
- 1/4t cayenne
- 1/2 ripe avocado chopped
- 1T extra virgin olive oil
- 2t minced fresh dill weed

WATERMELON GAZPACHO

serves 2–3

Refreshing and perfect for a summer lunch!

In a large bowl combine the watermelon puree with the diced vegetables, season, taste. Chill in the fridge for at least half an hour. Sprinkle with fresh black pepper. Garnish with a sprig of cilantro. Enjoy!

1 cup watermelon, de-seeded and puréed in a blender

1/2 cup de-seeded watermelon, diced

1/2 cup de-seeded tomato, diced

1/2 cup peeled, de-seeded cucumber, diced

1/4 cup yellow bell peppers diced

1 green onions minced

1/2t grated ginger

1/2 small jalapeño or green chili de-seeded and minced

1/4 cup mint minced

Handful cilantro (coriander) leaves minced

1T lime juice

1/2t Himalayan salt (to taste)

1/2t roasted cumin powder

1/4t chat masala (optional)

Sprinkle of freshly ground black pepper

MUSHROOM CAPPUCCINO SOUP

serves 4–6

When you need something nurturing and are battling the flu, this is a great soup! I love serving it nice and frothy like a cappuccino. This is inspired by the traditional miso soup. Miso is a fermented bean paste with a complex salty flavor. It is a superfood. Miso contains all the essential amino acids, making it a complete protein. It is rich in B vitamins, including B-12. Miso has probiotics and aids in digestion.

Blend all ingredients of stock until smooth. Marinate the mushrooms for at least 15 mins. Pour stock into serving bowls or cups and garnish with mushrooms, green onions & a drizzle of toasted sesame oil.

Variation: Can add sea vegetables like 1/4 cup hijiki and 1/4 cup wakame soaked, rinsed and drained. Both expand on soaking. Seaweed is rich in proteins and minerals.

Broth:

5 cups warm water
1/4 cup white miso
1T sesame oil
1T dulse flakes
1T grated ginger
Himalayan salt (to taste)

Shiitake Marinade:

1 cup shitakes, de-stem & sliced
1T olive oil
1T tamari
1T lemon juice

Garnish:

1–2 green onion chopped
Marinated mushroom
1T toasted sesame oil

SEAWEED SALAD

serves 3–4

Sea vegetables are high in nutrients, high in protein and iodine. This is missing from the western diet. Some of my favorites are nori, wakame, arame and hijiki which I have been experimenting in recipes from my time in Singapore.

Soak the seaweed in a bowl of water for a few minutes until it softens. Drain and pat dry on a towel and cut into 1/2 inch pieces. Mix the dressing in a medium bowl, and all the vegetables then lastly mix the seaweed and sprouts. Garnish with white sesame seeds.

1/2 ounce (handful) dried seaweed of your choice: arame, hijiki or wakame

2 carrots shredded

2 cucumbers julienned

2 green onions sliced

1 cup pea shoots or any sprouts in season

1 cup white bean sprouts

Handful of cilantro

Dressing:

2T tamari

1T raw sesame oil

1T lemon or lime juice

1T shredded ginger

1 clove garlic shredded

1t red bean sauce or red chili

1t toasted sesame oil

1T plum sauce (optional)

1/4t Himalayan salt (to taste)

KALE SALAD

serves 2

The trick to a great kale salad is to massage, marinate and wilt the kale so is easier to eat and digest. Is best at room temperature.

De-stem the kale leaves and cut into bite size pieces. If using lacinato kale, de-stem the kale then roll 2 leaves tightly like a cigar then cut into thin strips, this will chiffonade the kale. Place the kale in a large mixing bowl, add the olive oil, lemon juice salt and 1/4 cup of the avocado, then work the dressing into the leaves until they wilt. Add rest of ingredients, toss and mix well. Let marinate for 10 minutes at room temperature before serving.

1 bunch kale (lacinato or curly kale)

1 cup grape tomatoes sliced in half

1 large avocado diced

2T olive oil

2T orange juice

1 cup pomegranate seeds

1 cucumber sliced round

2 green onions sliced round

1T honey (optional)

1T pine nuts

1t Himalayan salt

1/2t cayenne (optional)

Dash of black pepper

GADO GADO

serves 4

An Indonesian favorite! These flavors take me back to tropical Bali. The vegetables just come alive with the sauce!

Blend the sauce, taste to flavor balance the tangy, salty and sweetness to your taste. Coat the serving bowls with the sauce. Distribute the vegetables evenly in the 4 serving bowls to look good. Garnish with cilantro, chopped cashews and dulse flakes.

Garnish:

1/2 bunch cilantro

1–2T cashew rough chop

1T dulse flakes

1 cup napa cabbage or spinach
2 ripe tomatoes quartered
1 handful of radish sliced
1/2 cucumber sliced round
1–2 handful beansprouts
1–2 red chilis sliced round
1–2 shallots sliced thin
3–4 organic eggs boiled, remove shell & sliced (optional)
2 potatoes boiled and cut into chunks (optional)
Dash of pepper

Sauce:

1 clove garlic
2T tamarind paste
2 small key limes juiced
2T tamari
1 cup peanut or almond butter
1T palm sugar (to taste)
1t Himalayan salt

VIETNAMESE SPRING ROLLS

serves 3–4

6 rice paper wrappers (8″ round Vietnamese dried rice paper)

6 Kale or lettuce leaves or nori sheets

3 green onions sliced lengthwise

1 ripe mango thinly sliced lengthwise

1 cucumber cut into thin strips 2″ length

1 carrot ribbons (with vegetable peeler)

1 red bell pepper cut into thin strips

1/2 cup loosely packed cilantro, large stems removed

1 cup alfalfa sprouts

Handful sunflower sprouts (optional)

Handful mint leaves

6t bon bon sauce

1/8 cup black sesame seeds for sprinkling

Moisten the edges of one rice paper in a large bowl, do not drop the entire sheet into the bowl as it will get soggy. The middle stays dry. Place one lettuce leaf in the center of the rice paper. Using the back of a teaspoon, spread 1 teaspoon of bon bon sauce on the kale or lettuce leaf. Start stacking the remaining ingredients lengthwise layering with the alfalfa sprouts on top. Careful not to over-stack. Fold 2 sides in and roll away from you, tucking as you go. Wrap & roll. Cut into half and sprinkle with black sesame seeds. Repeat until all 6 rolls are complete and serve with bon bon sauce.

These two recipes were inspired during my time at Living Light Culinary Institute in California.

BON BON SAUCE

makes 1 cup

The sauce is reminiscent of a spicy peanuty sauce that just brings the rolls to life!

Combine all the ingredients in a high-powered blender and puree until smooth. Add only as much water as needed to form a thick sauce. Store in a sealed glass jar in the refrigerator for up to one week.

1/2 cup raw tahini
2T grated fresh ginger
2T lemon juice
2T agave nectar
2T tamari
1/2t crushed garlic
1t red bean chili paste or red chili
Water as needed

PURPLE CABBAGE WRAP WITH GUACAMOLE

serves 2–4

Purple cabbage leaves

Grape tomatoes chopped

Handful cilantro roughly chopped

Guacamole:

2 ripe avocados

Juice of 1 lemon

1/8 cup de-stemmed cilantro leaves

1T dulse flakes

1/2 t Himalayan salt

1/4 cayenne pepper (optional)

1 green onion, chopped (green & white portion of stalk)

In a medium-sized mixing bowl, combine all except avocado. Whisk together gently. Add avocados, using a fork, gently mash them into the lemon mixture until slightly creamy texture forms. Use within 24 hours for best results.

Assemble just before serving. Lay the purple cabbage leaves on a flat surface. Spread 1 heaped tablespoon of guacamole. Garnish with tomatoes, cilantro and dulse flakes.

MUSHROOM WILD RICE

serves 2–3

Place the rice in a glass jar and fill to the top with water. Cover the jar and set in a warm area of the kitchen. Change water twice a day. The rice will begin to sprout or bloom. Sprouts within 2 days. Rinse and drain the rice well and transfer to a large bowl. Add all the vegetables to rice.

Combine the seasonings and oils in a small bowl and stir until well combined. Pour over rice mixture and stir until evenly distributed. Put into a heated oven already switched to low and warm for 30 minutes before serving. This will let the flavors meld. Store in airtight container in the fridge, will keep for 3 days.

1/2 cup wild rice

1/2 yellow bell pepper chopped

3–4 shitake mushrooms chopped & soaked in a little tamari

1–2 green onions chopped

1/4t grated ginger

1t sesame oil

1t toasted sesame oil

1/2t salt

1t tamari

1t red bean paste (optional)

MARINARA SAUCE

serves 2–3

Place all ingredients in the food processor fitted with the "S" blade and process until smooth. Scrape down the sides of the processor and mix well. Store in a sealed glass container in the fridge for up to 3 days.

2 ripe tomatoes chopped

1/2 cup sundried tomatoes, soaked in oil

1 red bell pepper chopped

2T extra virgin olive oil

1t dried oregano

1 clove garlic

Small handful of fresh dill

1T sundried tomato powder

1t palm sugar or maple syrup

1t Himalayan salt

Pinch of black pepper

ZUCCHINI FETTUCCINE

serves 2–3

Cut the zucchini into thin noodles using a vegetable spiral slicer or a vegetable peeler to create long ribbons or "fettuccine." Toss with olive oil and fresh herbs and serve with marinara sauce.

2 zucchinis, peeled

THAI GREEN CURRY

serves 4–6

Blend the coconut meat with water to make coconut milk, then add the rest of the ingredients, blend until smooth. Transfer into a bowl and add the cut vegetables. Dehydrate for 2–3 hours to warm the curry and let the flavours meld. Alternatively warm in the oven for 15–20 minutes.

Serve with kelp noodles (recipe on page 56) or with mushroom wild rice (recipe on page 51)

Cut Vegetables:

1 zucchini (w/skin) chop diagonal small 1/2 inch pieces

1 red bell pepper chop small 1/2 inch pieces

2 shallot sliced thin

3 green onions sliced round

1 zucchini (w/skin) roughly chopped
2t palm sugar
4 shallots
1/4 cup coconut meat or shredded coconut
1/8 cup mint leaves
Handful of cilantro
3T lime juice
1t tamari
1T sesame oil
5 keffir lime leaves, deveined & chopped
1/4 cup water
2T lemongrass stems chopped
Small handful of Thai basil
1 small garlic clove
1t shredded ginger
1t toasted sesame oil
1t Himalayan salt
1/2t coriander powder
1/2t roasted cumin powder

KELP NOODLES

serves 4–6

- 1–2 bags of kelp noodles
- Warm water
- 1t baking soda
- 1t lemon juice
- 1/4 cup tamari
- 1T olive oil
- 1T agave nectar

Kelp noodles are a seaweed and loaded with mineral rich nutrients. They have very little flavor but have a wonderful texture and take on the character of any sauce and soup. This is a great gluten-free raw option and lends itself well to all recipes that require a noodle texture.

Thoroughly rinse kelp noodles and place in a large bowl. Add water and baking soda and soak for 15 minutes. Rinse well. With scissors cut into small pieces for serving. Combine lemon juice, tamari, oil and agave nectar and stir into noodles. Allow to marinate for at least 1 hour or as long as overnight. Add to the Thai green curry. Put in serving bowls and garnish with fresh cilantro leaves.

SHAMI KEBABS

makes about 20

This dish reminds me of my grandmother. She always made the best! Hard to believe it is not meat. The walnuts make it hearty and the indian spices just meld together in this recipe!

1 cup dehydrated walnuts

1 cup sprouted mung

1 carrot roughly chopped

1 onion roughly chopped

1 celery stick roughly chopped

2 limes adjust w/taste

1/8 cup flax meal (1/16 cup mix, rest pat dry on patties)

1t salt to taste

1/4 cup beetroot juice

White pepper to taste

1/2t roasted cumin powder

1/2t chat masala (optional)

1/2t amchur powder (optional)

1/4t cinnamon powder

1/4t clove powder

Mix walnuts in a food processor, then carrots, celery, onions & sprouts. Add all other ingredients. Season and taste. Make into balls 1T each, pat dry with Flax meal, put on dehydrator sheets or oven baking sheets. For the Dehydrator: dehydrate for 2 hours then flip on mesh sheets for another 2 hours.

For the Oven: Heat oven to 200C then reduce to 50C, put kebabs in and warm for 20 minutes, flip and continue for 20 minutes more until moist in center but not dry.

(Photo on following page)

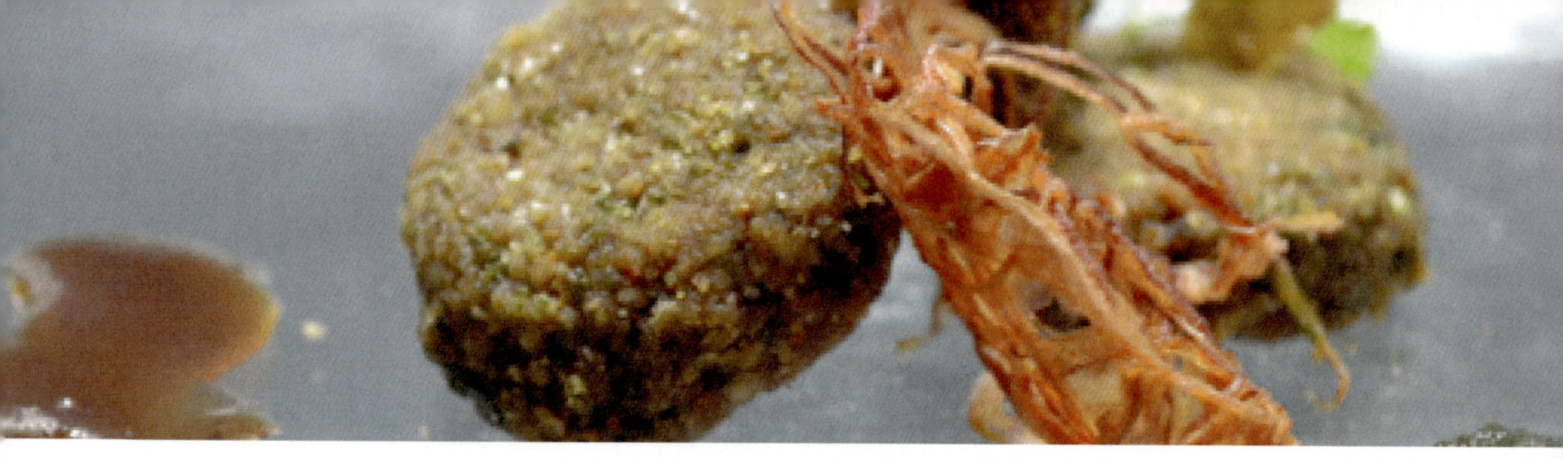

CILANTRO & MINT CHUTNEY

makes about 1/2 cup

- 1 bunch cilantro
- 1/2 cup fresh mint leaves
- 1 green chili
- 1/2t shredded ginger
- 1t lime juice
- 1t Himalayan salt
- 1/2t roasted cumin powder
- 1/2t coconut sugar
- 1/8 cup water to blend

In a blender, blend the above ingredients and adjust for taste. Add the water slowly, just enough to blend. Store in an airtight glass jar, keeps for 1 week in the refrigerator.

LETTUCE TACOS

serves 6–8

Spicy Beans:

- 1 1/2 cup sunflower seeds, soaked for 2 hours or more
- 1 cup sun-dried tomatoes, soaked for 1 hour or more
- 1T miso
- 2t ground cumin
- 2t ground coriander
- 1/2–1t cayenne pepper
- 2T olive oil
- 1T agave nectar
- 6T filtered water
- 3 green onions, chopped
- 1 small handful of cilantro
- 1/2–1 jalapenos, seeded & minced
- 1t Himalayan salt

Spicy Beans:

In a food processor, grind the sunflower seeds, tomatoes, miso, cumin, cayenne, coriander, olive oil, agave nectar and salt until thoroughly combined. Add the water a few tablespoons at a time and process for a wet dough-like consistency. Taste for seasoning. Add the jalapenos, green onions and cilantro and pulse for a few times to combine but leave small bits of cilantro. Spoon the mixture onto 1 or 2 Teflex-lined dehydrator trays. No need to smooth out; leave it chunky on the tray but flat enough to fit under another tray. Dehydrate at 115°F for about 3 hours or warm in the oven. The mix should be dry on the outside and not too mushy, so it can be broken up into pieces.

(*Photo on following page*)

LETTUCE TACOS

continued

Tomato Sauce:

Put all the ingredients into a food processor and grind well to a thick sauce consistency. Put the 'bean' mixture in a medium bowl and break any larger pieces. Add the tomato sauce and toss to combine well. It should be thick and somewhat spreadable. If not using right away, cover and store in the refrigerator, will stay for up to 5 days.

Sour Cream:

Put all ingredients into a blender and blend until smooth. The left over sour cream may be stored in the fridge for up to one week in a sealed glass jar.

Lay the lettuce leaves on a flat surface. Spread 1 heaped tablespoon of the spicy 'beans' and tomato sauce mixture on each lettuce leaf. Top with 1 heaped tablespoon of guacamole (recipe on page 50) and salsa (recipe on next page). Add 1 heaped teaspoon of salsa. Add a drizzle of 'sour cream' and garnish with alfalfa sprouts. Fold the sides to form a taco shape. Repeat with the remaining lettuce leaves.

Tomato Sauce:

1 cup sun-dried tomatoes, soaked for at least 1 hour

Sour Cream:

1 cup cashews, soaked for 1–2 hours

1/2 cup water

2T lemon or lime juice

1T light miso paste

1T nutritional yeast

Pinch of white pepper

Pinch of nutmeg

Pinch of Himalayan salt

SALSA

serves 6–8

In a medium bowl, combine the salsa ingredients and toss gently. Taste for seasoning.

2 roma or red tomatoes, seeded & finely diced

1 cucumber diced

1 green onion thinly sliced

1 small red onion minced

Handful cilantro chopped, packed

1/2–1 jalapeno or green chili seeded & minced

1T lime juice

1/2t Himalayan salt

fermented foods

great for the gut

CARROT KANJI

makes 1 gallon jar

This recipe is from my mother. Carrot kanji is a supertonic made from black carrots during the winter months. Tastes salty, tangy and spicy! But a half glass is all you need as this is a potent drink!

In a gallon glass jar, add all the ingredients then cover with water, leaving a few inches space from the top. Stir, mix well and put the jar in the sun for 4 consecutive days. When the kanji is ready, the color will deepen to a beautiful burgundy color and it will have a mature salty, tangy, spicy fermented taste!

Nutritional Note

This supertonic is loaded with antioxidants and probiotics, boosts the immune system, and warms up the digestive tract! But a glass is all you need, as this is a potent drink!

2 cups black or deep red winter carrots, peeled & cut lengthwise into 2" pieces

4T salt

1T red chili powder

2 1/2T mustard seeds ground coarsely

1/4t hing or asafoetida

1 gallon water

KOMBUCHA

makes 1 large glass jar

7 cups of water, divided

1/2 cup organic brown sugar

2–3t organic loose black or green tea

2 tea bags for color

1 cup brewed kombucha

Wooden spoon, muslin cloth, kitchen towel

1 kombucha tea starter SCOBY*

Boil 3 cups of water in a stainless steel pot. Add sugar and stir until dissolved. Stir with a wooden spoon. Remove from heat and allow to soak tea and cool for 30 minutes to room temperature. Strain through a muslin cloth.

Transfer to a large glass jar and add remaining water and previously brewed kombucha. Make sure to leave 1–2 inches of free space at the top of the jar.

ALWAYS WASH HANDS BEFORE HANDLING SCOBY*
Add scoby. Make sure not to use any metal when handling scoby.

Cover the jar with a cloth and secure with a rubber band to prevent fruit flies from getting into the scoby. Leave undisturbed for 7–10 days in a warm dark place. As your kombucha ferments, a new SCOBY will grow to the width of the container and attach to the original SCOBY.

*SCOBY: symbiotic colony of bacteria and yeast

KOMBUCHA

continued

After a week, sample your kombucha to determine if it is ready to drink. It should be a bit bubbly and taste both sweet and sour without much hint of the tea. If you are pleased with the taste, use clean hands to remove the SCOBY and place in a sealed glass container with a little brewed kombucha to cover and store in the fridge to make your next batch. If it is not ready, allow your kombucha to ferment until satisfied.

Transfer kombucha to glass jars for storage (swing-top bottles work well), leaving about 1/2 inch headspace at the top. Allow bottled kombucha to sit at room temperature for a day or two to ferment a bit more and build up carbonation, then place in refrigerator until ready to drink.

Kombucha will last in the refrigerator for up to 3 weeks, but it is best if consumed sooner.

CASHEW HERB CHEESE

serves 4

Nuts or seeds can make delicious cheeses. Always soak the nut or seed according to the soak chart, rinse and blend with probiotic powder, this ferments the cheese. You can flavor your cheese according to your tastes using spices or your favorite herbs.

- 1 cup cashew, soaked for 2 hours, rinsed & drained
- 1/2 cups purified water
- 2t light miso
- 2t nutritional yeast
- 1/2t probiotic powder
- 1/2t Himalayan salt
- 1/4t nutmeg
- 1/8t ground pepper
- Handful of fresh herbs minced

Combine cashews, water and probiotic powder in a blender and process until smooth. Add a small amount of additional water, if necessary to facilitate processing. However use as little water as possible to achieve a thick, creamy consistency. Line a plastic berry basket or colander with damp cheesecloth and set on a shallow dish. Pour the mixture into a bowl, cover with a cheesecloth and place in a warm location to ferment for 2–4 hours.

After 1–2 hours put a heavy weight on the cheese to help press out the excess liquid. Check the cheese every 2 hours and drain the excess liquid from the plate. Ferment longer if a stronger cheese is desired. After the cheese has fermented to your taste, mix rest of ingredients and set into a mould. Store in a sealed glass container in the refrigerator, will keep for 3–4 days. Can use garlic or scallions instead of mixed herbs.

LIVE SAUERKRAUT

makes 1 large jar

1 large head of cabbage

2t Himalayan salt

1t fresh minced dill

Save 1–2 big cabbage leaves. Shred rest of cabbage with a knife or food processor, wash and drain. Add salt and massage into the cabbage, wearing gloves. Keep massaging until it releases juice. Let stand for 10–15 mins and massage again for several minutes, repeat until cabbage is very juicy and covered in juice.

Pack the massaged cabbage and dill weed firmly into a larger jar. Press the cabbage down until its liquid rises to the top and covers it by at least 1/8 inch. Put a whole cabbage leaf and then a plate on top with a small glass jar filled with water. Cover with a clean dish towel. Ferment in a cool, dark place for at least 3 days, depending on desired degree of sourness. Remove any bubbling at the top of the jar each day. Make sure kraut is covered by liquid. Once kraut is ready, store in sealed glass jars in the fridge for several months

Can add cauliflower, carrot or beet and seasonings like garlic or ginger.

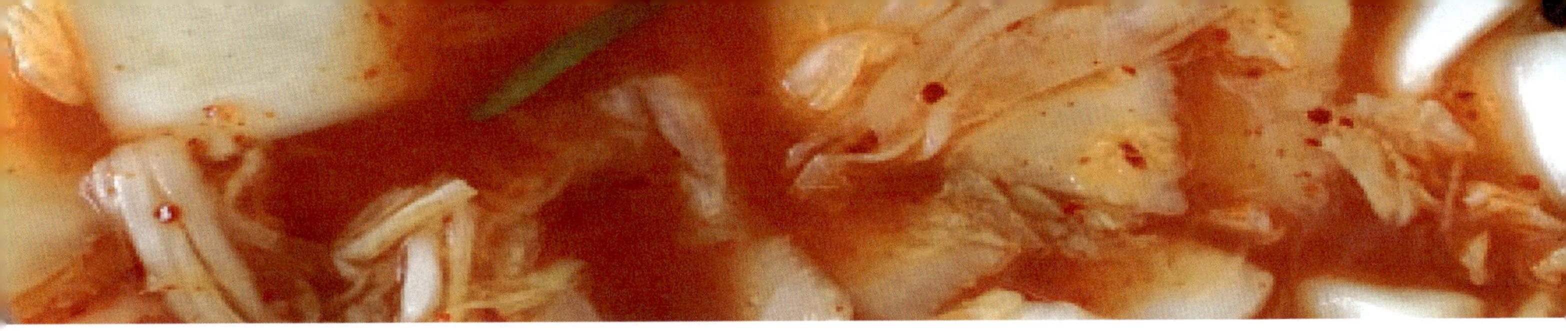

KIMCHI

makes 1 large mason jar

Place the napa cabbage and daikon pieces in a large mixing bowl. In a separate small bowl, mix salt in water and dissolve. Pour over the vegetables. Wear disposable gloves and massage into the vegetables. Add remaining ingredients and massage again. Set aside at room temperature for 3 hours to soften. Cover with a thin cloth over the bowl. Then transfer and tightly pack into a large mason jar, cover with cloth and lid and set aside at room temperature for 3 days. Leave space in the jar as kimchi will expand upon fermenting. Remove cloth, put lid on. Refrigerate. Will stay for 1–2 months in the fridge.

1 napa cabbage, washed,cut crosswise, 2 inch chunks

1/2 medium daikon radish, cut into 1/2 inch chunks

2T Himalayan pink salt or sea salt

2 green onions sliced into 2 inch lengths

1/2 cup water

3 cloves garlic shredded/minced

1T grated ginger

1T Korean chili powder (available at Korean stores)

2T maple syrup or natural sweetener of your choice

COCONUT YOGURT

serves 2–3

Coconut meat of 2 coconuts (medium thickness)

1/8 cup water

1/4t probiotic powder

1t coconut oil

Drizzle of honey or agave nectar

In a high speed blender, blend all the ingredients to a smooth consistency. Put into a glass mason jar, cover with lid and leave in a warm part of the kitchen to ferment. Will expand slightly. Sets overnight. Enjoy with berries and a drizzle of honey. Once fermented keep in the fridge for 3–4 days. Will continue to get stronger and more tart in the fridge everyday. Consume on the same day or make just a small batch.

raw desserts

they are simply divine

CHOCOLATE MOUSSE

serves 5

Cacao is raw, unprocessed coco with all the nutrients intact. Carob Powder is caffeine-free and contains 50% more calcium than cacao. I like to combine both powders for their amazing health benefits.

1 ripe avocado (cut and deseed)

1/4 cup young coconut meat (optional)

1/2 cup water

1/4 cup agave nectar or honey (adjust to taste)

1/2 cup made up of equal portions of carob & cacao powder (or coco)

1t vanilla extract

1/8t cinnamon powder

Pinch of Himalayan salt

Blend all except the avocado with water for even consistency. Add avocado and blend until smooth. Serve in dessert glasses and chill in the fridge for 30 minutes.

Note: Use ripe avocados for best results! The secret ingredient: Avocado makes it thick and rich, but it cannot be detected in the flavor.

MANGO CHIA PUDDING

serves 4–8

Blend all the ingredients except for the chia seeds in a blender until smooth. In dessert glass add 1–2T of chia seeds, pour the blended cream and stir until evenly mixed and let sit for 15 minutes or more until the chia seeds become a tapioca consistency. Chill in fridge for 30 mins. Garnish with fresh mango or dried fruits and nuts. Dust with a little nutmeg. This can be enjoyed for a delicious breakfast!

1/2 cup chia seeds

1 cup cashews soaked for 1–2 hours & drained

1 cup water

1 mango peeled & cut into chunks

1/4 cup honey (to taste)

1/2t cinnamon powder

1/4t nutmeg powder

1/4t ginger grated

1t vanilla extract

1 vanilla bean scraped

1/8t Himalayan salt

CHOCOLATE-COVERED STRAWBERRIES

for a box of strawberries

- 3–4T cacao powder
- 6T coconut oil, melted
- 3T maple syrup (to taste)
- 3/4t vanilla or orange extract
- Pinch of Himalayan salt
- Box of strawberries

Whisk all ingredients in a bowl except the cacao powder. Add cacao powder slowly, whisking until fully combined and smooth consistency. Attach toothpicks to the ends of strawberries and dip into chocolate sauce. Garnish with chopped nuts and put in the refrigerator for 10 minutes to set.

Nutritional Note

Raw cacao is one of the most powerful antioxidants on the planet! Rich in essential minerals, including magnesium, sulfur, calcium, iron, zinc, copper potassium and manganese, also good for heart health. Balances hormonal mood swings!

FLOURLESS CHOCOLATE CAKE

makes one 7–8 inch cake; serves 4–6

2 1/2 cups raw walnuts (unsoaked)

14 pitted medjool dates, unsoaked

1/3 cup cacao powder or unsweetened cocoa powder

1/3 cup carob powder

1t vanilla extract

6t water

1/4t Himalayan salt

1/2 cup fresh raspberries or strawberries for garnish

Place the walnuts and salt in a food processor fitted with the S blade and process until finely ground. Add the dates, cocoa powder and rest of ingredients and process until the mixture begins to stick together. Add the water and process briefly. Transfer to a serving plate and form into a 7–8 inch round cake. Decorate the cake with fresh raspberries or strawberries before serving. Covered with plastic wrap, the cake will keep for 3 days in the refrigerator or 2 weeks in the freezer. Bring to room temperature before serving.

Raspberry or Strawberry Sauce:

1 cup fresh or frozen raspberries or strawberries (thaw and drain, if frozen)

1/4 cup pitted medjool dates soaked

1/8 cup water

Variation with Raspberry or Strawberry Sauce: Place all the ingredients in a blender and process until smooth.

MEXICAN FLAN

makes 4 small dessert portions

Blend in a high-speed blender like a Vitamix, cashews, coconut meat and agave nectar until smooth. Add all other ingredients except the garnish. Blend until smooth but do not over-blend. Pour into a flan mould or any smooth-sided ramekin and refrigerate for 2 hours or longer until set. When firm, turn over and remove from ramekin. After plated, drizzle with 1t agave nectar already mixed with the carob powder. This gives a caramelized effect and sprinkle with a superfood such as bee pollen.

1/2 cup cashews, soaked for 1 hour

1 cup fresh tender young coconut meat

1/4 cup agave nectar or maple syrup

1/4 cup Irish moss paste (recipe on next page)

1 vanilla bean, scraped

1/4 cup melted coconut oil

1/8 cup water or fresh orange juice (add if fresh coconut meat is thick)

1t lemon juice

1t vanilla extract

1/4 t Himalayan pink salt

Garnish:

4t dark agave nectar or maple syrup mix with 1t carob powder

IRISH MOSS PASTE

makes 1/2 cup

Irish moss is an invaluable part of contemporary raw dessert preparation. It keeps the dessert light and acts as a binding and gelling agent at the same time.

1 handful dry Irish moss or 1/8 cup packed

Cold water, to soak & rinse as needed

Take 1 handful dry Irish moss and rinse thoroughly to remove any sand. Soak moss in cold water for 1–2 hours, drain and rinse well again. It expands to 3–4 times to its size. Do not soak too long as it will decrease its gelling potential. Blend all the moss, adding very little water at a time. The moss may vary in water content, so you may need less. You will create a paste that should be smooth and thick like an apple sauce consistency. Store in an airtight glass container for up to 1 week in the fridge.

NEAPOLITAN TART

makes 8-inch tart

Chocolate Coconut Crust:

Add all the ingredients and half the date paste into a food processor. Process until the crust starts to rise on the sides of the processor bowl. Stop machine, scrap down the mixture with the spatula to make sure nuts get well broken down. Once well integrated add remaining date paste. The crust should start holding together. Lightly grease the sides of the tart pan with some coconut oil. Cut baking sheet and put at bottom of pan. Distribute crust evenly on the bottom and sides of the pie pan and lightly compact by hand. Crust should rise about halfway up the pan. Chill crust in the freezer for 20 minutes. Keep in fridge until ready to be filled.

Chocolate Coconut Crust:

1 1/2 cups coconut flakes

3/4 cup almonds

1 1/2 ounces carob powder (weight)

4 ounces date paste (weight)

1T vanilla extract

1/8t Himalayan salt

NEAPOLITAN TART

continued

Vanilla Custard Filling:

In a blender, blend all except the coconut oil and lecithin until smooth. Stop the blender and add the coconut oil, irish moss paste and lecithin. Resume blending until well incorporated. Pour filling into pie pan with pie crust. Place in freezer to set, 1–2 hours or until middle of pie is firm to the touch.

Glazed Strawberries:

Leave the strawberries aside, mix all the ingredients to make a smooth glaze and then pour over strawberries.

Assembly:

Layer 1 1/2 cups of the glazed strawberries directly on top of the vanilla custard. Toss the remaining 2 cups of strawberries with the freshly made glaze. Push strawberries slightly into the filling. For best results, toss fruit with glaze immediately as the glaze will begin to gel right away. Layer glazed berries on top of tart. Set in fridge 20–30 minutes or until glaze has gelled.

Vanilla Custard Filling:

11/2 cups soaked cashews

1/2 cup coconut meat (4 ounce wt)

1T vanilla extract

1 vanilla bean (scraped insides only)

1/2 cup agave syrup or palm sugar

1/2 cup almond milk

1/8t Himalayan pink salt

1T maple syrup

1T lecithin

1/2 cup coconut oil

1/3 cup irish moss paste

Glazed Strawberry Topping:

31/2 cups sliced strawberries

1/8 cup irish moss paste

1/2 cup orange juice, 1/2t orange rind

1T agave nectar

Pinch of Himalayan salt

INDEX

ABOUT THE AUTHOR

Sunita Vira is a Raw Food Chef & Nutrition Educator. Founder of the Raw Food Center Chicago & Singapore, Sunita has been working with raw living plant based foods for over 17 years. Her goal is to help people integrate healthy eating into their lifestyle for vibrant health! Sunita loves to travel and study various cultures and their foods. She shares ancient wisdom from around the world as she crystalizes and simplifies important steps to bring healthy eating into your life.

Sunita is based in Chicago and conducts fun culinary programs, seasonal cleanses, and sought-after culinary wellness retreats at hidden gems in exotic locations around the world with a personal touch of love!

For more information and to subscribe to our newsletter, visit our website at www.rawfoodcentre.com. For culinary inspiration, follow us on Facebook and Instagram at @rawfoodcenter. Enjoy culinary demonstrations on our Youtube channel: RawFoodCenter.

TESTIMONIALS

WELLNESS RETREATS

"Thank you for bringing us all together and creating our collective India. Perhaps how we see the world or our place in this world. Perhaps how we feed ourselves or how we feed our soul. Perhaps simply how we relax into the ebb and flow of life. We are forever grateful!"

DR. AMIE JEW, Louisiana

"The India retreat was a great adventure—well-planned, well-conceived and pulled off with grace and creativity."

DR. ELLEN JACOBSEN, Chicago

"I attended Sunita's Raw Food Culinary Retreat in Bali in April 2016 and I had a truly amazing week. It was a perfect retreat and I came back refreshed, re-energized and inspired to incorporate Sunita's delicious recipes into my daily life and reap all the wonderful benefits of eating more raw food!"

MONIQUE JHINGON, Manila, Philippines

CULINARY PROGRAMS

"I have been fortunate to learn from Sunita and her delicious recipes are now part of my daily routine! I highly recommend everyone to participate in Sunita's programs. I am convinced that meal preparation is fundamental in attaining good health."

DR. CRISTINA TORRES,
Integral Alternative Medicine, Chicago

"I just wanted to thank you for the fantastic workshop today. It really opened my eyes to what can be done with raw food, and how delicious it is! That dessert just blew me away, but the rest of it was very, very good too! I really must try some raw ice cream soon!"

DEBORAH MOORE

"Thank you for a wonderful experience! I have never been as excited to start eating more vegetable and integrating raw food in my daily meals! Never imagined it could taste this good!!!"

MASHAEL AL SULAIMAN

"Thank you, Sunita. I really enjoyed the class Saturday. I made all the food last night for dinner. My family loved it! I look forward to more classes!"

JONNA ROBISON, Singapore

"I had a great time and enjoy the classes very much. Thank you for sharing your knowledge and passion! I'm very happy & more confident to continue more raw food diet and introduce to my family."

JESS CAROL D'SILVA, Singapore

"Truly exceeded my expectations! So many great recipes, good tips & demonstrations. The food is delicious! I loved the extra weight loss and feeling good! I highly recommend this to all!"

DARRELYN MARX, Chicago

SEASONAL CLEANSES

"To my surprise, in a month's time, I'd shed 5 lbs of weight and 2 inches in my waistline effortlessly while enjoying delicious recipes. With Sunita's raw food training, delicious, effortless, super-living, rejuvenating raw food preparations are within my reach daily in a matter of minutes."

DR. RADHA SUKHANI,
Northwestern Memorial Hospital, Chicago

"Sunita's cleanse program is by far one of the best things I ever did."

JODI SERIO, Chicago

"I really enjoyed my detox program with Sunita; I have a lot more energy to enjoy my family. Higher energy levels are priceless!"

STEPHANIE, Singapore

"Your recipes are fabulous, and I so appreciate how you have incorporated the meal prep into the Cleanse, so we have skills to continue with ease (unlike other cleanse/detox programs)."

KAREN JACOBSEN, Chicago

BOOK

"My kiddos and I tried making your cake last night—and if you could only hear the moans and screams of joy, it was the most delicious thing we have ever tasted. LOVE your book!"

JILL SALZMAN, Founder of The Founding Moms, Chicago

SPEAKING ENGAGEMENTS

"Sunita electrified the fourth grade with a healthy living demonstration, I would love to see her offer a camp based on health and cooking this summer. An excellent idea!"

THOMAS STEELE-MALEY, GEMS World Academy, Chicago

info@rawfoodcentre.com
www.RawFoodCentre.com
www.facebook.com/rawfoodcentre/
www.instagram.com/rawfoodcenter/
www.youtube.com (look up Raw Food Center)

NOTES

Made in the USA
Lexington, KY
30 December 2017